JO THOMPSON

Workplace Stress and the Law

TO THOMPSON

Workplace Stress and the Law

Scott Sullivan

Barrister
Barnards Inn Chambers, London

CLT Professional Publishing Ltd
A Division of Central Law Training Ltd

© Scott Sullivan 2000

Published by
CLT Professional Publishing
Stonehills House
Howardsgate
Welwyn Garden City
Herts AL8 6PU

ISBN 1 85811 245 1

Typeset by Saxon Graphics Ltd, Derby
Printed in Great Britain by Antony Rowe

Contents

Preface

If there is someone who has gone through their working life without a day's stress, I have yet to meet them. Indeed, conversations overheard on trains, and in bars and restaurants throughout the country suggest that if such a person exists they are a rare, perhaps endangered, breed.

That said, whilst most, if not all, of the workforce will have experienced stress at work at some stage, individual reactions to it are far from uniform. Even more divergent are often the opinions which are expressed about those complaints which proceed beyond the staff canteen and into the country's courts and tribunals. To some, an award of compensation to an employee with a stress related complaint is no more than the unjust enrichment of a malingerer. "If they really want to know about hard work, they should spend a day with me!" To others, it is the appropriate recognition of a genuine grievance and one no less important than a bad back or keyboard strained wrist.

Legally, the progression from the former to the latter of these two views has been slow, but nonetheless significant. As this text seeks to show, the wide ranging impact which stress in the workplace has is one which can no longer be ignored neither can it be pigeonholed as the refuge of the weak. The flow of claims into the courts will no doubt continue to increase, but they will be a trickle rather than a torrent. The floodgates are unlikely to be troubled.

Above all, and often against a background of media hype, what is necessary is an appreciation of the fact that claims based upon stress at work, in whatever forum they are brought, can only succeed upon strict legal foundations. They are not easy cases to win. It is hoped that this text will set out, albeit in brief form, the development of this area of law and the elements which will need to be established for such claims to enjoy the prospect of success. If it does no more than provide a touchstone for further research and debate however, it will have achieved an aim consistent with its modest length.

Scott Sullivan
Barnards Inn Chambers
January 2000

Table of Cases

Table of Statutes and Regulations

Chapter 1

The Extent of the Problem

Legal recognition of the importance of stress-related illnesses may have come late but given the increasingly dramatic impact which stress has upon the workplace was surely inevitable. The following statistics indicate just how important a problem stress is.

- Nearly two-thirds of the nation's workforce suffer from stress at work.[1] In a study of over 400 organisations, both in the public and private sector 17% of staff claimed to suffer from stress "very often", and a further 43% said that they experienced stress "quite often".
- In 1996 187 million working days were lost to absence due to sickness costing British industry £12 billion. This works out at an average of 8.4 days sick leave for every employee at a cost of £533 per employee.[2]
- Each year in Britain 30 working days are lost due to stress or mental, illness for every day lost to industrial action.
- In 1995 the British Safety Council reported that the second largest category of occupational disease is stress caused or made worse by work.
- In December 1998 a biannual survey conducted by the TUC found that workers worry most about stress.[3]
- The Health and Safety Executive's (HSE) survey of work related illness found that the two most common self-reported work-related illnesses were musculo-skeletal disorders and stress, depression or anxiety or stress-ascribed illness.[4]
- Psychological disorders are most common during the prime working ages of 24–44.

[1] MFS, *Personnel Today*, July 1995.
[2] Confederation of British Industry, April 1997.
[3] P. Kirby, "1998 survey of safety reps", TUC 0171–636–4030.
[4] SWI 1995 ascribed five million lost days to stress depression or anxiety and one million more to trauma. Each person suffering from one of these conditions reported taking an average of over 15 days off work each year. HSC.
(HSE Books ISBN 0 7176 1509 X.)

- In 1993 the British Heart Foundation reported that:
  — of all male absence from work is caused by heart and circulatory disease.
  — of all premature deaths of working people between 35 and 64 are caused by heart disease.
  — For a company of 10,000 employees the costs each year would be as follows:
  (1) £2.1 million in lost productivity from men and £340,000 from women due to heart disease.
  (2) 35 men and seven women will die due to heart disease.
  (3) 59,000 working days for men and 14,200 working days for women will be lost due to problems associated with heart disease.
- In a survey of absenteeism carried out by the Industrial Society in March 1993 entitled "Wish you were here" over half of the respondents felt that emotional/personal problems and stress either caused or contributed to absence despite a general reluctance to admit to the same on certification forms.
- A survey of 630 trade union safety representatives in 1997 showed that 67% of respondents reported that their management had taken no action to reduce workplace stress. A survey of trade union members in 1997 showed that 81% thought that stress was either a fairly serious or very serious problem for employees in their organisation. 72% thought that stress levels were worse than the previous year.
- A survey carried out among subscribers to *Employment Review* and *Occupational Health Review* revealed that 58% of respondents regarded stress as one of their firm's top three health at work priorities; a quarter felt that it was the most important health issue. Managing stress was predicted to be the fastest growing area of work for health at work teams over the next two years.
- In 1995 the Health and Safety Executive's Survey of Self-Reported Work Related Illness estimated that 279,000 people in Great Britain were of the opinion that they were suffering from work-related stress, anxiety or depression and a further 254,000 believed that they were suffering from an illness which had resulted from work-related stress.
- In 1998 MORI carried out survey for the HSE of 800 small and medium-sized employers in an attempt to establish a

benchmark against which it could assess the success or otherwise of phase three of the Good Health is Good Business campaign. This survey revealed that:

— 31% of those who consider stress to be a health risk consider it to be a "high" risk.

— 22% of all respondents felt that stress was poorly controlled in their workplace. This statistic meant that stress was felt to be the least well controlled of all workplace risks.

- In 1998 a survey of 500 members of the Institute of Directors selected at random showed that almost 40% of them felt stress was a major problem in their organisation. Of those respondents nearly 90% regarded working practices as a factor which could be affecting stress levels.

- At the end of 1997 unions had 457 work-related stress cases in progress nationwide.[5]

---

[5] "Focus on union legal services", Trade Union trends survey 98/4. TUC publications.

Chapter 2

Stress – What is it? What Causes it? What are its Effects?

What is stress?

Whilst this is predominantly a legal text it is simply not possible to consider the legal concepts without first attempting to understand the background against which they must sit. Moreover, from the point of view of both employer and employee alike, there is an obvious need to recognise the symptoms of stress, the conditions to which they might lead and what causes such symptoms in the first place. It is only when these are understood that effective measures can be taken to combat them.

Numerous definitions of stress abound. In their handbook *Hard Labour*[1] the London Hazard Centre defines stress as follows:

> "When the demands and pressures placed on individual workers do not match the resources available, or do not meet the individual's needs and motivations, stress can occur and endanger that person's health and well-being. In the short term stress can be debilitating; in the long term, stress can kill."

Further assistance in finding a definition of stress can be derived from the Health and Safety Executive's book Stress at Work – A Guide for Employers (HSE Books) which refers to it as:

> "…reaction people have to excessive pressures or the types of demands placed upon them. It arises when they worry that they cannot cope."

More recently, in its discussion document titled "Managing stress at work" the Health and Safety Commission has defined stress as follows:

> "Stress is the reaction people have to excessive pressures or other types of demands placed on them."

---

[1] The London Hazard Centre, *Hard Labour* (Stress, Ill Health and Hazardous Employment Practices) (1994).

In putting forward this definition (which it is suggested is the best yet available), the Commission was keen to emphasise that it was concerned with adverse reactions to the demands of the environment and therefore distinguish between pressures or challenges which may be stimulating and stress which is the reaction to too much pressure.

Consistent with its many definitions, there is a general lack of agreement about the meaning of the word "stress", and even if it should be used at all. Stress, pressure and strain are often used interchangeably and incorrect use of the word stress is common since it is used on the one hand to mean the demands and pressures which life places upon us and on the other to mean the extreme psychological and physical effects which those pressures can have upon us if they are too severe or if they last too long.

As long ago as 1946 Hans Seyle, the so-called "father" of stress research, carried out what was, in all likelihood, the first scientific approach to the analysis of the subject. He observed that there were three stages in a stress-related illness. First, the individual undergoes an *alarm reaction* in which an initial period during which his resistance is weakened is followed by *countershock* during which the individual's natural defence mechanisms become activated in an attempt to deal with the source of the alarm reaction. This is followed by a period of resistance where the individual's defence mechanism is most heightened and, if he is fortunate, it is able to beat off the stressful agent and thereby avoid any stress-related illness. If such attempts fail, however, the third stage will be reached, *exhaustion*, by which time the individual's natural (or conditioned) defence mechanism will have collapsed.[2]

More recently, the focus has been placed upon the impact of an individual's environment upon their mental and physical health[3] but the end result of the analysis is often the same, namely that every individual has a mental and physical state of equilibrium which they try to preserve. Where this equilibrium is threatened (by a stressor) the individual acts to attempt to restore the state of equilibrium and to the extent that they are successful, stress, or prolonged stress and therefore illness, is unlikely to result. This process forms the individual's *adjustment process*, his strategies for coping.

---

[2] See further, Earnshaw & Cooper, *Stress and Employer Liability*, Institute of Personnel and Development (1996).

[3] Lazarus R Sherwood Wheatley, *Patterns of Adjustment*, New York, McGraw-Hill (1976); Cox T *Stress*, Macmillan (1978).

Finally, it is important to recognise that not all stress is bad. A certain amount of pressure is needed to stay healthy and alert. As Hans Seyle has said, the only person without stress is a dead person.

What causes stress at work?

Physical surroundings

The physical surroundings in which people work are all potential stressors. Obviously those who work in dangerous surroundings, such as fire-fighters, certain factory workers, scaffolders etc are likely to feel stress as a result of the environment in which they work, but even in the relatively secure environment of an office, the way in which the working space is arranged, the furniture, lighting, temperature, noise, and even odours are all a potential cause of stress.

In *Waltons & Morse* v *Dorrington*[4] the Employment Appeals Tribunal held, dismissing an appeal by the employer, that it was an implied term of an employee's contract of employment that she would not be required to work in a "smoke-filled" environment. Whether or not the smoke directly impacted upon the employee's health or could be proved to be a risk to the same was not the point. It affected her welfare such that the employer who failed to take reasonable steps to prevent her from having to work in such an environment (even if that meant imposing a no-smoking policy in the office generally) was in breach of the employee's contract of employment and that accordingly, the finding that she had been constructively dismissed would be upheld.

Whilst an employer may not be surprised to read that factors such as light, heat, noise and even smoke represent potential causes of stress, recognising stressors in practice is not always as straightforward. The quiet, peace-loving employer entrusted with overseeing the health and safety of his employees may not appreciate how for some, for example, an overly quiet or isolated workplace will be just as stressful as a noisy or crowded one.

---

[4] [1997] IRLR 488 (EAT).

Workload

Increasing workloads mean that many employees are taking work home with them in order to meet the demands being made of them and this often impacts adversely upon their family life and increases the pressure upon the individual.

- A survey of more than 400 staff carried out by the Institute of Personnel and Development[5] found 54% claiming that they were unable to meet deadlines which had been set for them during the normal working day.
- The Institute of Management Services reported results of a survey carried out among 400 managers for the year 1995–96 as follows:
  - 47% of a sample of 1,100 managers found that their workload had increased from the previous year;
  - almost 60% claimed that they always worked in excess of their official hours in any one week and approximately 15% worked every weekend;
  - only 50% of the respondents looked forward to going to work;
  - 65% were of the opinion that their professional and personal lives were out of balance, the former greatly outweighing the latter;
  - office deadlines were identified as a key source of pressure.[6]

As a result of such increasing workloads, not only are individuals coming under increased pressure, but various studies suggest that long working hours can be directly linked to heart disease. As long ago as 1975, a study of light industrial workers in California found that individuals aged under 45 who worked in excess of 48 hours each week were twice as likely to die from coronary heart disease than those who worked a maximum of 40 hours each week.[7]

---

[5] *Personnel Today*, July 1995.
[6] Karen Charlesworth, IMS (1996).
[7] Breslow Lofthouse and Buell P, "Morality from coronary heart disease and physical activity of work in California", *Journal of Chronic Diseases*, II, 615–624 (1975). For a contrary point of view see Haffington, Maffey and Brentnall, "Working long hours and health", *British Medical Journal*, 308, 1581–2 (1994).

That illness caused by overwork is increasingly common is evidenced by the fact that in Japan there is actually a word for a sudden death from a heart attack or stroke brought on by overwork, Karoshi. The United Kingdom is no longer a stranger to incidents of Karoshi. In January 1994 Alan Massie, a junior doctor, collapsed and died in Warrington Hospital at the end of an 86-hour week having been on duty for seven of the previous eight days including two unbroken periods of 27 and 24 hours respectively.[8]

The direct and adverse impact which long working hours can have upon an employee's health was the cause of sufficient concern to lead to the recent European Union Working Time Directive.[9] In November 1996 the European Court of Justice (ECJ) rejected an argument put forward by the UK government under Article 173 of the EC Treaty that the Working Time Directive was unlawfully made.[10] The argument centred upon the contention that the Directive (adopted under Art 118A of the EC Treaty as a result of approval by qualified majority in the Council) was, in reality, concerned with the regulation of the rights and interests of employed persons, and not with health and safety matters. The ECJ rejected the challenge holding that the core concepts of "working environment", "safety" and "health", terms which appeared in Article 118A, should be given a wide interpretation. Accordingly, the ECJ found that, although the regulation of working time was capable of affecting employment conditions, the primary object of the legislation was health and safety.

The Working Time Regulations 1998[11] represent the main implementation of the Directive into UK law. These came into force on 1 October 1998 and provide workers with new minimum rights including, the right not to be required to work over an average of 48 hours per week, an entitlement to paid annual leave, weekly and in-work rest periods, and further special provisions for night workers.[12]

Somewhat paradoxically, whilst most might accept that an employee upon whom too many demands are placed may suffer from stress, an

---

[8] *Observer*, 10 April 1994.
[9] Council Dir (EC) 93/104.
[10] *United Kingdom* v *European Commission* [1997] ICR 443.
[11] SI 1998 No 1833.
[12] For further reading see Gwyneth Pitt & John Fairhurst, *Working Time*, Blackstore Press Ltd (1998).

employee of whom little is required may similarly suffer from stress through boredom, or the imposition of menial, repetitive tasks. Invariably this affects junior staff more than their senior counterparts, potentially resulting in a feeling of worthlessness, which may be rendered particularly acute if the lack of stimulation is coupled with poor promotion prospects.

Reducing staff numbers

Now more fashionably termed as "down-sizing", a reduction in staff numbers can lead to stress either because an individual is directly affected through redundancy (or that of a spouse or partner) or because of an increased workload brought about as a result of decreasing levels of staff.

New technology

It seems that no business or employer is immune from the need to keep pace with new technology. The continued increase in, and emphasis upon, e-commerce will do nothing to arrest this momentum. Against such a background of change it is important to recognise the stresses which often accompany the introduction of new technology into a workplace. First, even talk of the introduction of new technology may lead to the concern of redundancies. Second, and perhaps most crucially, is a feared or actual inability to cope with the new technology introduced (itself often caused by poor consultation and training policies). Third, whilst the individual may cope or adapt well to the new technology, it does not follow that his colleagues or employers will, as a result of which strains may be put on relationships and an unpleasant atmosphere created within the workplace. Thus, whilst the introduction of new technology into the workplace is often designed to relieve the burden on employees the opposite result is just as frequently achieved.

At a managerial level, stress may be activated not only in coping with the new technology and the affect which it has upon the business (including fellow employees) once it has been introduced, but the need, or perceived need, to keep up with on-going and often rapid developments in technology brings with it additional pressure. The fear of being left behind in a global marketplace is a real one. Indeed, managers in the United Kingdom are second only to those in Japan in acknowledging the pressure which accompanies the need to embrace new technology and "keep up to speed".[13]

Career development

For many, perhaps the majority of employees, employment is seen as a ladder to climb. Promotion is the greatest form of approval and consequently something for which individuals constantly strive. It follows that the lack of opportunities for career development within an organisation can lead to frustration and stress, particularly as with promotion comes an almost inevitable increase in salary.

Reaching a ceiling in their career development is frequently cited by employees as a reason why they are unable to enjoy their work and are therefore more prone to stress. This may be particularly so of employees in their middle years who are not only the group most likely to find that their career progression has slowed or stopped altogether, but are also likely to be most affected by stresses in their home and personal lives.

Allied to the lack of opportunity for career progression is the fear of losing one's job. Again this may be felt particularly keenly by those in middle age who often regard their more junior colleagues as a threat rather than a challenge. Needless to say tensions of this type may affect the whole workforce if a poor working atmosphere is thereby created.

Just as the inability to advance one's career may result in stress, so the same result may be achieved by promoting someone beyond their own actual or perceived ability. Many organisations are guilty of placing the wrong people in the wrong jobs, more often than not due to an improper evaluation of someone's skills. The result can leave the individual feeling unable to cope with the tasks required of them, and therefore under pressure. Should those tasks involve the supervision of others this can cause additional pressures both for the individual and those whom they are supposed to supervise.

Role

Employees may suffer from role ambiguity, being unclear as to the tasks which are actually required of them, both from their employers and their co-workers.

---

[13] Earnshaw & Cooper, *op cit*, fn 2, *supra*.

Similarly, employees may experience role conflict, that is to say the feeling of being forced to carry out tasks which they do not want to or which upset or offend them in some way. Sometimes these tasks stretch beyond what they understand to be required of them and to that extent is allied to the question of role ambiguity. The need for an employee to strike a balance between quality and quantity or even safety is often far from easy, and is seldom free from stress. Attempting to perform such mental gymnastics or simply having to try and cope with an inability to do so, has been linked to sickness absence and job dissatisfaction.

Office politics

Where, within an organisation there are poor working relationships between employees *inter se* and between employees and management a low level of trust often develops, coupled with a sensation of isolation and lack of support. All are obvious stress factors. In a survey carried out by the Institute of Management Services[14] office politics was identified as a major source of stress at work.

The other side of that coin is that for those in managerial and supervisory positions stress may result from a failure to create a good working relationship between or with those beneath them or from an inability to delegate effectively, resulting in an increased workload.

In many companies the admission of being under pressure or suffering from stress is perceived as a sign of weakness. Accordingly, staff are reluctant to complain for fear that they will be regarded as unsuitable for the job or passed over for promotion. This reluctance is increased in times of high unemployment. Moreover, there are clearly occasions where poor working relations between employees or management and employees go beyond merely the creation of a bad atmosphere and manifest themselves in harassment or bullying. Although many companies (particularly large companies) are alive to the problems of bullying and racial and sexual harassment and have policies designed to meet individual complaints, the tendency to complain only as a last resort, particularly if the complaint is being made against a member of the management or involves a sexual allegation, should not be ignored.

---

[14] Karen Charlesworth, fn 6, *supra*.

Fear/trauma

Many employees work in situations where they are in fear of raids (and even personal attack) by criminals. This is particularly acute in jobs where the employer's business involves the handling of large sums of cash, *i.e.* post offices, banks and building societies, or jobs where the place of work is notorious for being a target of such attacks, *i.e.* convenience stores and off licences. Ironically, in attempting to combat crime through the installation of CCTV and video-phone links, employers may only have created a new Orwellian cause of stress with employees feeling that "big brother" is always watching them.

Witnessing or being involved in such an incident may well lead to psychiatric injury (including Post Traumatic Stress Disorder) and affect not only the individual but also his family.[15] In this context the case of *Frost* v *Chief Constable of South Yorkshire*[16] warrants some consideration. The case concerned representative claims brought by four police officers who had been on duty during the Hillsborough disaster but not in the immediate area where the deaths and injuries to spectators had occurred. Accordingly, the police officers could properly be categorised as secondary victims within the test laid down in *Alcock* v *Chief Constable of South Yorkshire Police*.[17] The House of Lords held that the duty which the defendant owed to the police officers as their "employer" was not sufficient to impose liability upon him for the (agreed) psychiatric injury suffered by them where, but for that relationship, they would not have recovered damages.

Of course, the fear need not be of attack by others. In *Francis Aston* v *ICI*[18] Rose J held that an employee was entitled to recover damages for psychiatric illness which was the result of a build up of anxieties caused by a fear of the safety of his place of work. The claimant had been exposed to Vinyl Chloride Monoma between 1970 and 1974, a carcinogen causing angiosarcoma of the liver but

---

[15] As many as 15% of all "front line" London ambulance staff suffer from PTSD (COHSE 1993). The Essex Police conclude that a substantial minority of British police officers may be experiencing psychological stress as a result of their operational duties: Jennifer Mitchell-Gibbs, "Occupational trauma in British police officers", Essex Police HQ, Springfield.

[16] [1998] 3 WLR 1509 (HL(E)).

[17] [1992] 1 AC 310.

[18] Transcript, 21 May 1992.

which the claimant had been told had a latency period of 15 years and once contracted was likely to be fatal within six months. In giving judgment Rose J stated:

> "It seems to me that the driver of a car whose speed and manner of driving are such as negligently to terrify his passenger to the extent of psychiatric illness is just as liable as the driver who physically injured his passenger by impact."

Impact of stress on businesses and individuals

Impact on business

Productivity

Not only will productivity be reduced due to lost working days caused by stress-related absences but even when employees are actually at work, given the high percentage of them who are likely to be affected by some form of mental illness of impairment (estimated by the Industrial Society to be in the region of 20%) productivity will be reduced as stress prevents an individual from performing at his or her best and may even have a "knock-on" effect upon the capacity of colleagues, either because they are dragged or simply slowed down by the employee so affected.

Morale

A low level of morale is likely to result from stress among employees leading not only to lower efficiency rates but also to a lack of pride in the product being produced or service offered. Customer relations will obviously be put at risk, again jeopardising productivity.

High staff turnover

It is almost inevitable that employees who are unhappy with their employer or finding it too difficult to cope at their job will look for another or give up working altogether. The result is that the employer loses a valued and trained worker and will be faced with the costly exercise of hiring and training a replacement. Of course, the departure of an individual employee may have a destabilising effect on the work-force generally, leading to further departures, a general feeling of unease in the workplace and engenders a lack of loyalty from employees to their employer.

Impact on employees[19]

Behavioural symptoms
- irritability
- indecisiveness
- frustration
- inability to concentrate
- lack of focus
- tearfulness
- lethargy.

Physical symptoms
- lack of appetite
- twitches
- nausea
- headaches
- cramps
- fainting and dizzy spells
- difficulty breathing
- disturbed sleep patterns.

Illnesses linked to stress:
- coronary heart disease
- asthma
- suppression of the immune system[20]
- rheumatoid arthritis
- gastric and peptic ulcers
- bronchitis
- intestinal problems[21]
- thyroid disorders
- skin diseases[22]

---

[19] Cooper CL *Handbook of Stress, Medicine and Health*, Boca Raton, Florida CRC Press (1996).

[20] Fox B H, "Premorbid psychological factors" *Journal of Behavioural Medicine*, Vol I(I) (1978); Cooper C L & Watson, Maffey & Brentnall, *Cancer and Stress: Psychological, Biological and Coping Studies*, Chichester, John Wiley & Sons (1991).

[21] Quick J C & Quick J D, *Organisational Stress and Preventative Management,* New York, McGraw-Hill (1984).

[22] *Ibid.*

- obesity
- tuberculosis
- headaches and migraine
- diabetes
- impotence and frigidity.

Social impact
- drug abuse and addiction
- increased cigarette and alcohol consumption
- breakdown in personal relationships
- violent assaults on others
- accidents.

Chapter 3

Stress as a Personal Injury Action

Negligence is the principle cause of action in an employer's liability claim. Although the relationship between an employer and his employees is necessarily a contractual one, it has been conclusively established that concurrent duties exist in both contract and tort and that an employee may sue in either.[1] In practice, an action in the latter will almost invariably be the more attractive, avoiding, as it does, the need to consider remoteness of damage and periods of limitation (in contract, time runs from the breach of warranty rather than the date when the damage was sustained).

Whilst an action in negligence is to be preferred, the contract of employment may nevertheless be relevant in considering whether or not the employer is in breach of duty. A breach of the implied duty of good faith, or of an agreed disciplinary procedure may be a cause of stress to the employee and it will be difficult for a employer to establish that he was acting reasonably if he acted in breach of such a contractual obligation. In fact, the formulation of an employer's duty of care is closely associated with the contract of employment or employment relationship.[2]

Moreover following the case of *Johnstone v Bloomsbury Health Authority*[3] it is unlikely that a court will uphold a clause in an employee's contract which means that he is effectively exposed to a system of work which will cause him or others potentially serious harm.

Of course, where the claim is one of bullying or victimisation the claim may well be in tort but not negligence. Instead the action would properly be founded in nuisance or trespass to the person.

---

[1] *Matthews v Kuwait Bechtel Corporation* [1959] 2 QB 57.
[2] See *Wilson and Others v West Cumbria Health Care NHS Trust* [1995] PIQR P38.
[3] [1991] 2 WLR 1362.

Common law framework

The general nature of the duty owed by an employer to his employees was described by Lord Wright in *Wilson & Clyde Coal Co Ltd* v *English*[4] as follows:

> "I think the whole course of authority consistently recognises a duty which rests on the employer and which is personal to the employer, to take reasonable care for the safety of his workmen, whether the employer be an individual, a firm, or a company, and whether or not the employer takes any share in the conduct of the operations. The obligation is threefold, as I have explained [*i.e.* 'the provision of a competent staff of men, adequate material, and a proper system and effective supervision']"

It should be noted that this decision was delivered at a time when the doctrine of common employment was still in existence (it was abolished by the Law Reform (Personal Injuries) Act 1948) and accordingly, at a time when an employer would not be liable where an employee suffered injury as the result of a negligent act of a fellow employee engaged in common employment. Today, the duty which the employer owes is a single personal duty.[5] Moreover, the duty is non-delegable so that the employer is under a duty to ensure that care is taken by all of those persons whom it employs.

That the duty is a single, personal duty and therefore owed to each of his employees individually is of some importance in the present context as it involves the employer having to consider and take account of any peculiarity or particular weakness of the employee. According to Lord Simonds in *Paris* v *Stepney BC*,[6] an employer's

> "liability in tort arises from his failure to take reasonable care in regard to that particular employee and it is clear that, if so, all the circumstances relevant to that employee must be taken into consideration."

If, however, the employer is unaware of the particular weakness or susceptibility of a particular employee then he may well escape liability on that ground. The relevance of whether an employer was aware of a particular employee's susceptibility to injury or illness will be returned to in considering the case of *Walker* v *Northumberland County Council*.[7]

---

[4] [1938] AC 57 at 84.
[5] *Wilson* v *Tyneside Window Cleaning Co* [1958] 2 QB 110 at 123–124.
[6] [1951] AC 367 at 375.
[7] [1995] 1 All ER 737.

Although a single personal duty, the scope of an employer's duty can be divided into five categories:[8]

(1) To provide a safe place of work, including a safe means of access.
(2) To employ competent servants.
    Now that the doctrine of common employment has been abolished this is of less importance. However, the court has found employers liable to compensate employees for bullying by work colleagues.[9]
(3) To provide and maintain adequate plant and appliances.
(4) To provide a safe system of work – a term used to describe:
    ● the organisation of the work
    ● the way in which it is intended the work shall be carried out
    ● the provision of adequate instructions
    ● the sequence of events
    ● the taking of precautions for the safety of the workers and at what stages
    ● the number of such persons required to do the job
    ● the roles of each employee
    ● the moment at which they shall perform their respective tasks.
(5) Other cases including vicarious liability for damage caused by other employees and the protection of employees from criminal attacks.

In any workplace it is not only an employer who owes duties to employees, employees owe duties *inter se*. Two or more employees working for the same employer owe a duty to each other to take reasonable care and are liable to each other for damage which the other suffers as a result of the failure to carry out that duty. Whilst this has only found judicial interpretation in the context of physical injuries, it may well be possible to argue that an employee, in a managerial role, who places undue pressure upon a subordinate employee or who fails to properly supervise that employee has failed to discharge that duty and may therefore be liable to them.

---

[8] *Charlesworth & Percy on Negligence*, 8th ed, (1990) 10–13.
[9] *Veness v Dyson, Bell & Co* [1965] CLY 2691.

Statutory framework

There is no specific legislation on controlling stress in the workplace. Pursuant to section 2 of the Health and Safety at Work Act 1974, however, an employer is placed under various legal duties designed to secure the health, safety and welfare of his employees.

The general duty placed upon an employer is contained in section 2(1) which states that an employer must "ensure so far as is reasonably practicable the health, safety and welfare at work of all employees". More specific duties are contained in the sub-sections which follow. Of these, the most significant as far as stress is concerned would seem to be:

- Section 2(2)(c) which obliges an employer to provide information, instruction, training and supervision so as to ensure employees' health and safety.
- Section 2(2)(e), which obliges an employer to provide and maintain a working environment that is safe and without risks to health.
- Section 2(3) which requires an employer of more than five employees to draw up a written policy statement on health and safety at work, and to bring it to the attention of all employees.

Whilst breach of any of these provisions will not give rise to any civil liability, the Health and Safety at Work Act 1974 is enforced (including by criminal prosecution) by the Health and Safety Executive (HSE) through its inspectorate. Indeed, the HSE is active in attempting to raise awareness of the causes of stress at work and the steps which can be taken to alleviate it. In particular, the HSE has published a short booklet, *Stress at Work: A Guide for Employers*[10] which, although relatively brief in its treatment of the subject, does illustrate the importance the inspectorate will attach to the mental as well as the physical health of employees.

Aside from the general duties laid down in the Health and Safety at Work Act 1974 there a number of other regulations which might be of application to an action based on stress at work. Of these, the Management of Health and Safety at Work Regulations 1992 is surely that of most general application.

---

[10] Suffolk, HSE Books 1995.

By virtue of regulation 3.

> "(1) Every employer shall make a suitable and sufficient assessment of –
>
> (a) the risks to the health and safety of his employees to which they are exposed whilst they are at work; and
>
> (b) the risks to the health and safety of persons not in his employment arising out of or in connection with the conduct by him of his undertaking,
>
> for the purpose of identifying the measures he needs to take to comply with the requirements and prohibitions imposed upon him by or under the relevant statutory provisions ..."

There is no reason why the risk assessment should not include the mental as well as physical health of the employees. Indeed, if it failed to so it would be out of line with Article 2 of the Framework Directive.[11]

In carrying out such an assessment, whilst an employer may be entitled to assume that its workforce is capable of withstanding reasonable pressures at work, where it fails to take into account factors about a particular employee which are known and which would render that employee less likely to be able to withstand such reasonable pressures, it is unlikely that an employer will be found to have carried out a "suitable and sufficient" assessment. When considering capabilities and training an individual employees specific vulnerabilities are again brought into focus.

By virtue of regulation 11:

> "Every employer shall, in entrusting tasks to his employees, take into account their capabilities as regards health and safety. An employer who knows of an individual employee's susceptibility to stress and stress related illnesses will therefore be required to take these factors into account when allocating duties at work."

Thus, whilst there are no specific statutory provisions governing stress at work (and are unlikely to be any for the foreseeable future) reference may be made to the Health and Safety at Work Act 1974 and the Management of Health and Safety at Work Regulations 1992 for

---

[11] EC Dir 89/391.

general duties owed by employers to their employees. Neither of these imposes a civil liability upon the employer but their breach will be evidentially probative. Moreover, other regulations may be of more specific assistance. Noise is dealt with under the Noise at Work Regulations 1989. Room dimensions, seating arrangements and lighting are all covered by the Workplace (Health, Safety and Welfare) Regulations 1992. Welfare facilities, fresh air, temperature and weather protection and lighting are within the scope of the Construction (Health, Safety and Welfare) Regulations 1996.

Finally, as mentioned above, the Working Time Regulations 1998 set down a maximum weekly working time (48 hours), lengths for night work, provision for the health assessment and transfer of night workers to day work, pattern of work, rest periods, annual leave. A detailed analysis of each of these regulations is beyond the scope of this text. Suffice to say that where stress has been suffered, it will often be possible to identify a breach of one of these statutory provisions.

Chapter 4

Walker v Northumberland County Council

On 16 November 1994 Colman J delivered a judgment[1] which was treated in the media, and legal circles, as something of a landmark in the recognition of stress as a condition for which an employer might be found liable to his employees. More recently, in *Lancaster v Birmingham City Council*[2] attention was again focused on workplace stress through a case in which the employer, for the first time, admitted liability for a stress-related injury to its employee. In reality, the seeds for both of these decisions had been sown several years earlier.

Johnstone v Bloomsbury Health Authority

The plaintiff in this case[3] was a junior doctor employed under a contract which required him to work 40 hours each week and to "be available" for an additional 48 hours per week on average. Having fallen asleep at the wheel of his car and careered off into a tree following a 110-hour working week the plaintiff resigned and commenced an action against the Health Authority alleging that it was in breach of its duty as his employer to take all reasonable care for his safety and well being. Further, the plaintiff sought a declaration to the effect that:

- he could not lawfully be required to work under his contract of employment for a continuous period of more than 24 hours without a break of at least eight hours;
- he could not lawfully be required to work under his contract of employment for so many hours in excess of his standard working week as would foreseeably injure his health, notwith-

---

[1] [1995] 1 All ER 737.
[2] Unreported.
[3] [1991] 2 All ER 293.

standing that in consequence the total number of such excess hours worked by him might have amounted on average to less than 48 hours a week.

In dealing with various appeals which came before it on interlocutory rulings made by courts below, the Court of Appeal made it clear that although the Health Authority had a discretion under the plaintiff's contract to require him to work up to 88 hours each week, it could not exercise that discretion in a manner which would present a reasonably foreseeable risk that the plaintiff's health would be injured. The Court of Appeal indicated that if the facts alleged by the plaintiff were made out, the defendant Health Authority would be in breach of duty.

Of particular interest in the present context is that the plaintiff was claiming that he had been required to work intolerable hours which had resulted in him suffering from stress and depression and had led to thoughts of suicide. He is quoted as saying:

> "I felt as though I had a bad case of 'flu or jet lag a lot of the time. The exhaustion made me clumsy – I'd often spill my food or drink. I felt like I was unconnected to my body, empty, like a squeezed out tube of tooth-paste. I experienced feelings of unprovoked hostility towards my colleagues, especially if they were making new demands on me. Worst of all, despite having entered medicine out of compassion and desire to help sick people, I found myself resenting the patients. I began dreading each day. Over the months I got more and more ground down, getting increasingly desperate and wondering at times if I might be better to be dead."

Gillespie v Commonwealth of Australia[4]

Gillespie, the plaintiff, a former Australian diplomat made a claim against the Australian Foreign Affairs and Trade Department for damages for a mental breakdown which he suffered as a result of the stresses created by living in Caracas, Venezuela where he had been posted. The plaintiff maintained that the stress to which he was subjected could have been avoided or at least reduced if the defendant had sent him on a training course prior to his posting.

[4] (1991) 104 ACTR 1.

The plaintiff's claim failed. It was held that although the magnitude of the harm suffered was considerable, there was not a high degree of probability that harm of that kind, or intensity, would eventuate. Some risk of psychiatric harm was foreseeable but the plaintiff's particular vulnerability (over and above that of other diplomatic staff in Caracas) was not and that even if the defendant had warned the plaintiff of the risks there was no evidence that he would not have accepted the post, or had he done so, avoided his mental breakdown.

Petch v Customs and Excise Commissioners[5]

The plaintiff here was a civil servant who, by 1973, had risen to the rank of assistant secretary. In 1974 whilst working in the defendant's department, the plaintiff suffered a nervous breakdown. In 1975 he returned to work but, prior to being transferred as assistant secretary to the Department of Health and Social Security, suffered from a bout of hypomania. In 1983 he again fell ill but was able to return to work until 1986 when he was retired from the civil service on medical grounds. In a claim for damages the plaintiff alleged that his illness had been caused by the volume and stressful nature of the work which he was required to undertake by his employers.

In giving evidence, however, the plaintiff said that it was not so much the volume of work which he was required to carry out as much as the conflict in roles or conflict of conscience which he considered that he had been placed in by his superiors. Indeed, numerous witnesses in the case testified to the fact that the plaintiff appeared to revel in the workload and that he was the last person whom they felt would suffer a nervous breakdown.

As far as his breakdown in 1974 was concerned, Dillon LJ held that unless senior management were aware or ought to have been aware that the plaintiff was showing signs of impending breakdown or were aware or ought to have been aware that the work which he was being asked to carry out presented a real risk that the plaintiff would have a breakdown, his employers were not negligent. Dillon LJ accepted that once the plaintiff returned to work in 1975 the duty which his

---

[5] [1993] ICR 789.

employers owed to him included a duty to take reasonable care to ensure that the tasks which were required of him were not such as to bring on a second breakdown. That said, a bout of hypomania in 1975 could not be attributed to any breach of such duty on the part of the plaintiff's employers the conduct of whom Dillon LJ found to be worthy of commendation.

Walker v Northumberland CC[6]

The facts:

- Walker was aged 50 and worked for the Council from 1970 until December 1987.
- Walker held a middle management position and was responsible for the management of four teams of social services field workers in the Blythe Valley area.
- Blythe Valley had a high incidence of child care problems, particularly abuse cases.
- Walker was responsible for holding case conferences in respect of these child care cases.
- During the 1980's the workload for the department increased but no additional field workers were employed.
- Between 1984 and 1987 Walker complained to his superiors about increasing work levels and the inability of his field teams to cope.
- In 1986 Walker suffered a first nervous breakdown and was absent from work until March 1987.
- Prior to returning to work Walker requested assistance but when he returned the assistance actually provided was temporary and inadequate and Walker was faced with a backlog of work which had built up during his absence.
- The number of child care cases continued to increase after Walker's return.
- In September 1987 Walker was diagnosed as suffering from stress-related anxiety and advised to go on sick leave.
- Walker suffered a second nervous breakdown and in February 1988 was dismissed on grounds of permanent ill health.

---

[6] [1995] 1 All ER 737.

Having found there to be "no logical reason" why the risk of psychiatric damage should be excluded from the scope of an employer's duty of care or from the co-extensive implied term in Walker's contract of employment, Colman J went on to consider the liability of the defendant for each of Walker's two breakdowns.

The first breakdown

In adopting the reasoning of Dillon LJ in *Petch*, Colman J indicated that the question which he had to ask himself was whether the Council:

> "ought to have been foreseen that Walker was exposed to a risk of mental illness materially higher than that which would ordinarily affect a social services middle manager in his position with a really heavy workload. For if the foreseeable risk were not materially greater than that there would not, as a matter of reasonable conduct, be any basis upon which the council's duty to act arose. It is therefore necessary to ask whether, prior to his first breakdown in 1986 there was anything in Mr Walker's conduct or any information about his work which ought to have alerted the council ... to the fact that Mr Walker was reaching breaking point or at least was subject to a materially greater than ordinary risk of mental breakdown."

On the facts of the case Colman J found that:

- There was no evidence that the Council had previously encountered mental illness in any of its offices with a similarly heavy and difficult workload to those in Blythe Valley.
- There was nothing in Walker's conduct or representations about staffing levels and lack of resources which would have suggested that he was at breaking point or that he was at serious risk of mental illness.
- Generally, there was no evidence that Walker was at any materially greater risk of stress-induced mental illness than any other area manager of a similarly busy area would be.
- It was not reasonably foreseeable to the Council that the workload to which Walker was exposed gave rise to any material risk of mental illness.

The second breakdown

In respect of the second breakdown Colman J found as follows:

- Before his return in March 1987 Walker had made it clear that he could not manage the Blythe office without additional support.
- In those circumstances the Council ought to have foreseen that if Walker was again exposed to the same workload as prior to his first breakdown there was a risk that he would suffer from further mental illness of such severity as would likely end his career as an area manager if not in social services altogether.
- In fact, the workload increased and no additional permanent assistance was provided.
- By April 1987 Walker was exposed at work to a reasonably foreseeable risk to his mental health which materially exceeded the risk to be anticipated in the ordinary course of an areas officer's job.
- The standard of care required of a reasonable local authority required that when Walker returned to work in March 1987 he would be provided with additional assistance and his workload permanently reduced.
- Walker made it clear to the Council that he could only return to work with assistance and that in choosing to continue to employ him without providing such assistance, it acted unreasonably and so was liable for Walker's second breakdown.

The *Walker* case went to the Court of Appeal. In its notice of appeal the Council's main contention was that as it was a local authority administering resources, the test which should be used in determining liability was not the "employer's liability" test but rather the equivalent of the *Wednesbury* reasonableness test, *i.e.* was the failure on the part of the Council so unreasonable that no reasonable authority would have behaved in the way that the Council actually did? And further, did the Council fail to take into account any relevant consideration or alternatively take into account irrelevant considerations in deciding upon the allocation of resources? Mr Walker cross-appealed against the finding of Colman J that the first breakdown was not reasonably foreseeable. In the event the claim was settled for £175,000.

Chapter 5

The Law after Walker

As a result of the decision in *Walker*, the elements necessary for a claim based on stress at work to enjoy prospects of success would appear to be as follows:

The employee must identify a duty which the employer was under, whether at common law or pursuant to statute

Except in situations where the alleged stressor is a physical or environmental one (in which case as seen earlier, reliance upon more specific statutory provisions may be possible) the two duties most commonly relied upon will surely continue to be the common law duty to provide a safe system and place of work and the duty under regulation 3 of the Management of Health and Safety at Work Regulations 1992.

There is considerable judicial agreement as to the formulation of the general duty which employers owe to their employees in the particular context of stress at work. In *Walker*,[1] Colman J put it thus:

> "where it was reasonably foreseeable to an employer that an employee might suffer a nervous breakdown because of the stress and pressures of his workload, the employer was under a duty of care, as part of the duty to provide a safe system of work, not to cause the employee psychiatric damage by reason of the volume or character of the work which the employee was required to perform."

In *Petch*,[2] Dillon LJ endorsed the concession made by counsel for the defendant that

> "The Defendants owe the Plaintiff a duty to take reasonable care that the duties allocated to him should not damage his health. She further conceded that the duty extended to his mental as well as physical health, subject to a caveat that foreseeability and causation were likely to be more difficult issues in mental injury cases such as this."

---

[1] *Supra*, p26.
[2] *Supra*, p25.

The employee must establish that the employer has been in breach of this duty

This will almost certainly be the most difficult constituent to prove. As in all claims in negligence whether or not there has been a breach will depend upon the magnitude of the risk of injury (a combination of the likelihood of some injury on the one hand and the severity of it on the other) and the steps necessary to alleviate it. It is a classic balancing act. Accordingly, where the incidence of stress-related injury is high and the consequences severe, then the magnitude of risk is also high and the employer will be required to go to considerable lengths to alleviate that risk. Where, however, the incidence of stress-related injury is low, so that although the consequences may be high the magnitude of the risk is not, so the measures required of an employer will be reduced.

The courts appear ready to accept that the consequences of stress related injury are severe. In both *Gillespie*[3] and *Petch*[4] the courts seem to have assumed that mental breakdown was undoubtedly severe. Likelihood of injury, however, will not be so assumed and will continue to be the hurdle which the majority of stress-related claims fail to surmount. In *Walker*,[5] certain, perhaps unusual, features, enabled the claim to succeed but these are unlikely to be common place. Establishing that the employer should reasonably have foreseen the injury which the employee has suffered is likely to come either from:

- knowledge of a particular employee's vulnerability; or
- the nature and extent of the work itself.

Knowledge of a particular employee's vulnerability

Such knowledge may be either actual or constructive. Actual knowledge will be rare, probably existing only in cases such as *Walker* and *Petch* where the employee has been the victim of a previous

---

[3] *Supra*, p24.
[4] *Supra*, p25.
[5] *i.e.* Walker was of normal character, he suffered two breakdowns, there was extensive documentary evidence of complaints and concerns from Walker and social workers generally, there was clear evidence of causation, the employers promised Walker support but did not deliver any.

nervous breakdown, or where there is a history of recorded absences for stress-related illnesses. In this context it is worth noting that whether an absence is self-certified or supported by a medical report the word "stress" will have to be expressly stated. A medical certificate to the effect that the employee is suffering from a stomach complaint may well be another way of expressing that an employee is suffering from a stress-induced ulcer but if it is, and the employer is to be fixed with actual notice of an employee's particular vulnerability, the report should say so explicitly.

If the culture in the workplace is such that the employee feels unable to make known the true reason for his illness this may be an approach which is easier to preach than practise. Whether or not an employer has sufficient systems in place to enable grievances to be aired and complaints made will obviously fall to be considered in determining the steps necessary to alleviate the risk of injury. Indeed, it is likely to be one of the first matters which the court would expect any employer to have addressed.

More prevalent (and more difficult to prove) will be cases where the employer is alleged to have constructive, rather than actual, notice of the employee's condition. An employee's dress, demeanour and his general level of performance may all be adversely affected such as should put the reasonable employer on notice that the employee is at risk of suffering from a psychiatric injury. Is the employee frequently absent from work? Has he become withdrawn, hostile or tearful? Has he increasingly missed deadlines or produced poor quality work? Of course, an affirmative answer to these questions, even to all of these questions, will not necessarily lead to the conclusion that the employee is at risk of impending psychiatric harm, but an employer who neglects to consider this as a possibility may well be held to have constructive knowledge of a particular employee's vulnerability.

The nature and extent of the work itself

To date, it has proved difficult to succeed on an allegation of an excessive workload alone. Indeed, the distinction between a claim based upon this and one in which the employee is said to have actual or constructive knowledge of the particular vulnerability of an employee (irrespective of the nature or level of the work required of him) can be illustrated by reference to two recent cases.

In *Maryniak* v *Thomas Cook Ltd,*[6] Mr Maryniak was a branch manager employed by the defendant who complained that his depression was the result of negligence on the part of the defendant. He alleged that the defendant knew that he was suffering from work-related stress and anxiety but did nothing to assist. Instead, it was said that there was a policy to destroy his career. Although it was accepted that the defendant knew that the claimant had attended his general practitioner he had not been diagnosed as suffering from any stress-related illness and there was nothing in his behaviour at work to suggest that he was suffering from stress. Accordingly, his claim was dismissed.

The contrary position can be seen in the case of *Lambert* v *Liverpool City Council,*[7] Mr Lambert worked for the City Council's Highway Department and alleged that he was overworked which had caused him to suffer from psychiatric illness resulting in three periods of absence. He maintained that he had complained to the Council about the level of work which was being required of him but that it had done nothing to improve matters and had even failed to operate its own sickness procedure. Finally, Mr Lambert was retired on grounds of ill health. His claim was settled by the Council in the sum of £92,000.

Is such a distinction justified? In *Walker*, whilst Colman J accepted that stress leading to psychiatric damage may be caused to a normally robust person by the nature and the volume of work required of him, he nevertheless continued to say that:

> "the circumstances in which claims based on such damage are likely to arise will often give rise to extremely difficult evidential problems of fore-seeability and causation. This is particularly so in the environment of the professions, where the plaintiff may be ambitious and dedicated, deter-mined to succeed in his career in which he knows the work to be demanding, and may have a discretion as to how and when and for how long he works but where the character and volume of the work given to him eventually drives him to breaking point. Given that professional work is intrinsically demanding and stressful, at what point is the employer's duty to take protective steps engaged ? What assumption is he entitled to make about the employee's resilience, mental toughness and stability of character, given that people of clinically normal personality may have a widely differing ability to absorb stress attributable to their work?"

---

[6] [1998] CLY 358.
[7] Unreported.

In the opinion of Colman J, in circumstances where the Council had not previously encountered mental illness in any other of its area officers, it was not under a duty to take protective steps to prevent harm to Walker unless it ought to have foreseen that he was under a materially greater risk than his colleagues.

In respect of a claim based upon events in the mid 1980's this may be an appropriate test to apply but in the current climate would an employer be treated so favourably? The ability to point to either previous complaints made by the claimant, or to colleagues who, to the knowledge of the employer, had suffered in similar circumstances to the claimant will undoubtedly be the safer route to success. Surveys highlighted earlier in this text indicate the prominent role which stress has to play in absences from work through illness.

Indeed, the sheer number of these surveys and the coverage which stress continues to generate in the media, suggests that an employer who had overworked an employee might do well to escape liability simply on the grounds that the claimant's illness was the first which had been reported to it or that the claimant was the first employee who had fallen ill as a result of the demands placed upon them. This will especially be so if the employer failed to heed the sort of advice contained in the HSE guidelines on how to arrange working practices so as to minimise the risk of stress.

It is in this area that the impact of the Working Time Regulations may be seen most clearly. As stated earlier, the European Court of Justice has now declared that working time is a health and safety issue.[8] In a particularly interesting passage of his Opinion Advocate General Leger expressed the view that without the guarantees of the Directive, workers are exposed:

> "to the risk of frequently being required to work excessively long hours beyond their physical or psychological capabilities, thereby jeopardising their health and safety."[9]

In making its objections to the ECJ the UK government appears to have acknowledged that there is good scientific evidence that night shift work exposes workers to significant risks to their health and safety but at the same time argued that no such reliable evidence exists

---

[8] *United Kingdom* v *European Commission*, supra, p9.
[9] At para 103.

as far as the length of hours in day work is concerned.[10] The statistics reproduced at the beginning of this text suggest that this argument lacks conviction.

The magnitude of the risk of injury is just one half of the equation in establishing breach; the other is the steps necessary to alleviate that risk. The magnitude of risk may be great but where, as in *Petch*, the employer took all reasonable steps to counteract it, it will not be found liable if injury results. The steps which an employer should have taken will obviously depend upon the facts of the individual case and expert evidence may well be required (on the incidence of stress-related illness in the employee's particular field of employment as well) but some general indicators can be given.

- As far as is possible the employer should take reasonable steps to **design** the job so as to avoid stress (*i.e.* avoiding overtime, shift work, too great an emphasis on performance-related pay, sharing responsibility, particularly for decisions concerning health and safety).
- Care should be taken over the **physical surroundings** (*i.e.* heat, noise, pollution).
- An employer should seek to **avoid situations** where the employee is placed in a position of conflict, ambiguity, where he feels trapped (perhaps due to a lack of flexibility).
- An employer should provide **proper training** to *all* staff (including management).
- Accepting that however well designed a job and a workplace may be, stress is probably inevitable and an employer ought to assist employees to counteract stress including through the provision of **stress management training** and **counselling** should such training fail.
- Stress management training and counselling can only succeed if an employer has created a **culture** in which seeking assistance is not seen as a sign of weakness and an obstacle to career development. This will inevitably involve a **complaints procedure**, possibly outside of the usual management structures.

---

[10] In *Barber and Others* v *RJB Mining, The Times*, March 1999, Gale J held that the right to insist on working no more than an average of 48 hours taken over a 17-week rolling reference period is a term of each employee's contract. Note that leave to appeal was sought and granted.

- Allied to the need for a complaints procedure is the fact that none of the measures highlighted above will succeed without effective **monitoring**.[11]

It will be noted that the preventative steps listed above are not dissimilar to those which would be required of an employer faced with the risk of a physical injury, say, Repetitive Strain Injury. Indeed, employers and those advising them would do well to treat the risk as if it were a physical one and then simply adapt the necessary preventative measures which would be taken to deal with the risk of physical harm as appropriate.

The claimant must show that he has suffered a specifically definable illness caused directly by his work

Causation is a matter of fact and it is factual rather than legal problems which are likely to arise in establishing causation. In law, provided that some injury can be foreseen it does not matter whether the precise nature and extent of that injury was foreseeable.[12] This is the same whether one is dealing with physical or psychiatric illness. Following the case of *Page* v *Smith*[13] the "eggshell personality" is a principle of no less application than that of the "eggshell skull". According to Lord Browne Wilkinson,[14]

> "(An eggshell personality) is of no significance since the defendant did owe a duty of care to prevent foreseeable damage, including psychiatric damage. Once such duty of care is established, the defendant must take the plaintiff as he finds him."

Whilst earlier chapters have indicated the wide-ranging impact which stress may have upon an individual's health however, proving that coronary heart disease or rheumatoid arthritis have been *caused* by stress at work may still prove to be a difficult task. For this reason the majority of successful claims based on stress at work are likely to

---

[11] A failure to consider these factors may well result in the employer being in breach of reg 3, Management of Health and Safety at Work Regulations 1992.
[12] *Smith* v *Leech Brain* [1962] 2 QB 405.
[13] [1995] 2 All ER 736.
[14] At 754A.

continue to involve a recognised and diagnosed mental as opposed to physical illness.

Whether the illness is mental or physical, problems at home or in an employee's personal life associated with non work-related factors may only serve to complicate matters. A stress-related illness will often be multifactorial and it will only be if the employer can establish that his employer's breach of duty has made a material contribution to the cause or exacerbation of his illness will he recover.[15]

The volenti defence

Even if an employee is able to establish that an employer is in breach of the duty which it owes to him and that that breach has caused him harm, that may not be the end of the story. If an employee who has been absent from work due to stress voluntarily returns to work in the knowledge of the systems which are or are not in place and of the workload which he will face, arguably he has agreed to a system of work that may cause him further injury. Put simply, there is no legal duty upon an employer to decline to employ an adult employee for work which that employee is willing to do because the employer thinks that such work would not be in the employee's best interests. According to the decision in *Withers v Perry Chain Co Ltd*:[16]

> "if the common law were otherwise, it would be imposing a restriction on the freedom of the individual, and would be oppressive to the employee by limiting his ability to find work rather than beneficial to him. Moreover, there was no duty at common requiring an employer to dismiss an employee rather than to retain him in employment and allow him to earn his wages, because there might be some risk. If there was a risk it was for the employee to weight against the desirability or necessity of employment. The duty of the Defendants here was to take reasonable care of the Claimant in the employment on which he was engaged, having regard to the fact that she had dermatitis."

In *Walker* the Council did not raise this potential defence although it would no doubt have failed on the facts of that case as the Council had promised greater assistance to Walker should he return to work.

---

[15] *McGhee v National Coal Board* [1973] 1 WLR 1; *Bonnington Castings v Wardlaw* [1956] AC 613.
[16] [1961] 1 WLR 1314 (headnote).

Indeed, it was only on that basis that he had agreed to do so. Policy dictates that the occasions on which such a defence will succeed are likely to be few and far between.

The new claims

Whilst the majority of claims for workplace stress are, perhaps, always likely to emanate from overwork (and more likely to succeed in circumstances where the individual employee has previously complained about being under stress, but his complaints have not been properly addressed), two potentially discrete areas of liability have continued to develop.

Bullying

The majority of cases for bullying and harassment are likely to arise under the race and sex discrimination legislation[17] which impose a type of vicarious liability which is wider in its scope than that at common law.[18] Bullying and harassment at work may also constitute a criminal offence under either the Offences against the Person Act 1861 (OAPA) or the Protection from Harassment Act 1997.[19] At common law, where the conduct complained of has been of such seriousness as to render the employer negligent or in breach of its duties to its employees, it is difficult to imagine that the court will not also accept that such level of bullying would not lead to a foreseeable risk of mental harm.

In *Kirk* v *Nacano*[20] a multinational company settled an action commenced by a former employee who claimed that abuse and humiliation which had been visited upon him on a daily basis by a managerial team led to a nervous breakdown and an inability to continue working. It is a pity that this claim did not proceed to trial as it may have established new guidelines as far as foreseeability is concerned. Unlike in *Walker*, Mr Kirk had no prior history of mental illness and,

---

[17] See pp 50–52.

[18] *Jones* v *Tower Boot Co Ltd* [1997] ICR 254 (CA).

[19] In *R* v *Ireland and Burstow* [1998] AC 147 the House of Lords held that where the defendants were alleged to have made repeated telephone calls consisting of either harassment or heavy breathing this could constitute an offence under ss 18, 20 and 47, OAPA 1861 (and therefore also a common assault).

[20] (1998) December 1998.

at least until very close to his eventual breakdown, had seemed to thrive under the regime which his superiors had created. Perhaps even more crucially, Mr Kirk had not reported his ill health to his company. Indeed, the only factor on Mr Kirk's side was that a superior of his (but not one of the "bullies") had himself left the company claiming to be unable to continue to put up the abuse and humiliation. Mr Kirk had reported his on-going complaints to this individual but not, it would seem, whilst that person was still an employee of Nacano, to which no formal complaints had ever been made.

On the limited information which is available it is difficult to judge whether Mr Kirk or his former employers, or either, derived the greater benefit from the settlement. Suffice to say that Nacano was sufficiently concerned for its position (or possibly just the adverse publicity which a trial would likely generate) to settle Mr Kirk's claim for some £200,000.

In June 1998 the case of *Ratcliffe* v *Dyfed County Council*[21] similarly settled out of court for a sum of just over £100,000. The claimant was a head teacher who claimed that she had been bullied by another member of staff and had suffered psychological injury as a result. It is not clear whether or not the classic *Walker* ingredients of a previous known illness and complaints to the employer were present in this case.

Finally, in *R* v *Kellam, ex parte South Wales Police Authority*[22] Mr Justice Richards dismissed an application for judicial review of a decision by the police pensions medical referee that a particular officer qualified for an injury award under the Police Pensions Regulations.[23] The officer in question had retired from the police force because of stress caused by victimisation he received at work after his wife, also a police officer, had made allegations of malpractice in her unit. Mr Justice Richards found that the stress had been received in the execution of the officer's duty within the meaning of the Regulations.

Re-deployment
In July 1999 the case of *Lancaster* v *Birmingham City Council*[24] was the subject of extensive media attention when the claimant, Mrs

---

[21] Unreported.
[22] *The Times*, 24 August 1999.
[23] SI 1987 No 257.
[24] Unreported.

Lancaster, was awarded £67,000 in damages against her former employers. In fact, liability had been conceded in 1998. The facts of this case are as follows.

In 1978 Mrs Lancaster had become a senior draftsman in the architecture department of the defendant Council and in 1990 was promoted to procedures officer. In 1993, however, Mrs Lancaster's internal position was abolished and, without consultation, she was appointed to the position of housing officer. This represented a shift in career to a position for which she had no experience or qualifications. She maintained that this was effectively a "front line" post which involved dealing with disgruntled tenants whose attitude was said to have ranged from demanding to hostile. Mrs Lancaster was unable to cope and, after several periods of sick leave, was ultimately discharged.

It is not clear from the reports which were produced in the national press whether or not the award which Mrs Lancaster received related to the period commencing prior to her first period of absence, or not. If it did, and she had not complained of the difficulties which she was experiencing prior to falling ill, this case would appear to represent a shift from the position in *Walker*. If, though, the damages which she received were a result simply of the fact that, following her first, second, or third periods of absence, the council had failed to take any steps to alleviate the difficulties which Mrs Lancaster was experiencing then the award (and the admission of liability) would appear to do little more than rehearse the stance which Colman J had adopted in *Walker*.

Chapter 6

Stress as a Cause of Action in Employment Law

In the context of employment law, allegations of mental illness and stress are most likely to be a relevant factor in claims involving unfair, including constructive, dismissal and potentially under the new disability discrimination legislation.

Unfair dismissal

It is potentially fair to dismiss those employees who are unable to do their job properly due to ill health just as much as it to dismiss those who are simply incompetent.[1] Moreover, that an employee has a perfect record of attendance does not mean that he cannot still be fairly dismissed on grounds of capability. As we have seen, however, stress has been linked to any number of physical and psychiatric conditions such that it is likely that an employee suffering from stress may spend periods, even lengthy periods, away from work. Given that the Employment Appeals Tribunal has ruled that the principles relating to the dismissal of absentees apply as much to someone suffering from mental illness as they do to someone suffering from a physical ailment[2] it is necessary to consider absenteeism at work as a ground for dismissal in further detail.

In general, being absent from work without permission amounts to misconduct and therefore represents a potentially fair reason for dismissal pursuant to section 98(2)(b) of the Employment Rights Act 1996 (ERA). That said, a single absence will not normally amount to gross misconduct unless is a specific rule to that effect or it would clearly amount to gross misconduct.[3] In fact, there is no hard and fast rule as to the number of unpermitted absences which may

---

[1] Employment Rights Act 1996, s 98(2)(a).
[2] *Commissioners of Inland Revenue v Green* [1977].
[3] *Ross v Aquascutum* [1973] IRLR 107.

entitle an employer to terminate an employee's contract of employment. Each case must be judged on its own merits[4]

There is though a distinction between cases where the employee is suffering from an underlying medical condition: the "long term absentee", and that where the employee is absent on frequent occasions but due to different complaints, the "persistent absentee". It is possible that an employee suffering from stress may fall into either of these two categories. In whichever category an employee falls, it will be necessary for the employer to follow a fair procedure before he can legitimately dismiss the employee. Whilst the Act does not distinguish between the two categories of absentee, decided cases have revealed that a different approach may well be required by an employer seeking to investigate and ultimately dismiss an employee with a poor record of attendance.

The persistent absentee

A general explanation of the steps which are required of an employer faced with a persistent absentee can be found in the decision of the EAT in *International Sport Co* v *Thomson*[5] to the effect that:

> "where an employee has an unacceptable level of intermittent absences due to minor ailments, what is required is firstly that there should be a fair review by the employer of the attendance record and the reasons for it; secondly, the appropriate warnings should be given after the employee has been given an opportunity to make representations. If there is no adequate improvement in the attendance record, in most cases, the employer will be justified in treating the persistent absences as a sufficient reason for dismissal."

- An employer is obliged to investigate properly the facts including reviewing the employee's attendance record and any pattern emerging therefor and the reasons given for the absences.[6]
- An employer should interview the employee and obtain his explanation for the absences.

---

[4] *Newalls Insulation Co Ltd* v *Blackman* [1976] IRLR 303.
[5] [1980] IRLR 340.
[6] *Ibid.*

- In general terms when one is dealing with the persistent absentee there is often no connection between the illnesses complained of on individual occasions. In such situations it may well be impossible for the medical examiner to arrive at any sort of prognosis for the future. Where the absences are stress-related, however, it would probably be wise for the employer to explore whether or not the employee is suffering from any underlying medical condition.
- An employer should issue a warning to the employee that his level of attendance is unacceptable and what consequences may ensue if there is no improvement.
- Even having carried out the steps set out above, before actually dismissing an employee an employer will usually wish to consider the following factors:
  — the nature of the employee's illness
  — the likelihood of it or some other illness recurring
  — the length of various absences
  — periods of good health in between absences
  — the impact of the absences on others and the employer's business
  —what warnings had been given to the employee[7]

It will be appreciated that following any dismissal, large organisations should usually allow the employee an opportunity to appeal the decision to dismiss.[8]

The long term absentee

Although it may still be fair to dismiss an employee who is suffering from a long term illness, employers should adopt a different procedure in respect of an employee who suffers from an underlying health condition. In such cases the more appropriate consideration is not whether the conduct of the employee justifies dismissal but whether or not he is able to perform the tasks required of him following a serious illness or as a result of a serious condition.

---

[7] *Lynock v Cereal Packaging Ltd* [1988] IRLR 510.
[8] *West Midlands Co-operative Society v Tipton* [1987] IRLR 112.

- The overall aim of the procedure should be to obtain as much information about the employee's condition as is necessary to assess the situation properly.
- An employer should therefore ask the right questions, such as:
  — will the employee make a complete recovery and if so when?
  — is it practical to wait for the employee to return to full health?
  — if the employee is unlikely to regain full health will any residual disability affect his ability to perform the tasks required of him?
  — if the employee is no longer suitable for the position which he held prior to his absence is their any other position which he might be able to fill?
- In order to answer these questions the employer will almost certainly have to carry out.
  — a medical review
  — a consultation with the employee. In the present context this may be of particular importance. Say, for example, that an individual is suffering from physical ailments brought on by stress but that that stress is the result of the physical environment or working conditions of the employee, only by interviewing the employee will the employer be able to understand properly the root cause of the illness (and therefore the absenteeism).
  — where in the present context a consultation with the employee or other review carried out by the employer results in the identification of certain stressors the employer may be required to consider whether or not there are any practical steps which could be taken to alleviate the stress which the employee is suffering from.
    Whilst the duty upon employers to adopt a fair procedure and act reasonably is unaffected by the fact that an employee's absence was due to an injury caused at work,[9] a failure to take reasonable steps to eliminate or alleviate the stress is likely to result in a finding of unfair dismissal.[10]

---

[9] *London Fire and Civil Defence Authority* v *Betty* [1994] IRLR 384.
[10] *Piggott Bros* v *Jackson* [1991] IRLR 301.

Such steps may include altering the physical environment, *i.e.* elimination of excessive noise, light, heat, pollutants, the provision of extra assistance to meet with a demanding workload, the move to another department, moving or dismissing another employee guilty of harassment or bullying.
— take medical advice and arrange for an examination of the employee.

Constructive dismissal

By virtue of section 95(1)(c) of the ERA 1996 an employee may complain that he has been constructively dismissed in circumstances where the conduct of the employer is such that it entitles them so do. The Court of Appeal has made it clear, however, that a constructive dismissal claim will only arise where an employer can be shown to be in fundamental breach of a term of the employee's contract of employment.[11]

In considering the question of stress in the workplace, aside from any express terms that may exist in any one employee's contract, there are three implied terms of crucial importance:

(1) Duty to take care of an employee's health and safety

In the same way that an employee can claim damages in personal injury litigation, an employee who has been exposed to an unreasonable workload, or a stressful working environment can also complain that the conduct of his employer amounted to a breach of contract.[12]

(2) Duty to protect an employee from harassment, bullying or victimisation from work colleagues

Harassment does not have a discrete legal definition. In 1991 the European Commission adopted a Recommendation on the Protection

---

[11] *Western Excavating (ECC)* v *Sharp* [1978] IRLR 27.
[12] See, for example, *Johnstone* v *Bloomsbury Health Authority, supra*, p17.

of the Dignity of Men and Women at Work and a Code of Practice on measures to combat sexual harassment. This defines sexual harassment as:

> "unwanted conduct of a sexual nature or other conduct based on sex affecting the dignity of women and men at work including the conduct of superiors and colleagues."

The Commission for Racial Equality prepared similar guidelines on racial harassment at work, defining it as:

> "unwanted conduct of a racial nature, or other conduct based on race affecting the dignity of women and men at the workplace."

The parameters of what is and is not harassment, however, have been developed through cases under the Race Relations Act 1976 (RRA) and Sex Discrimination Act 1975 (SDA). In particular, it has been held that:

- Harassment need not be physical but can consist simply of insults and even body language.
- It need not be a continuing process; a single act can still constitute harassment although it is more usual to find the harassment occurring over a longer period of time.
- The acts complained of do not need to have necessarily occurred at the place of work or during normal working hours.[13] In claims under the SDA and RRA it will be noted that the acts must have caused the applicant some detriment and have taken place "in the course of employment" although this has been given a rather wide interpretation.

Like harassment, there is no precise legal definition of bullying and it too may take various forms, including physical assaults. Typically, bullying is alleged in circumstances where the employee complains of unfair and excessive criticism, being undervalued, being placed under excessive pressure or having unnecessary demands made of them.

Of course, a claim to constructive dismissal on grounds of harassment will only succeed where the employee has drawn the harassment to the attention of management and nothing is then done about it.[14]

---

[13] See *Van Den Bergen* v *Nabarro Nathanson* [1993] IRLR where an incident of sexual harassment occurred at an office Christmas party.

[14] *McCabe* v *Chicpack Ltd* [1976] IRLR 38.

Where an employee has been the victim of racial or sexual harassment by a fellow employee then that act of harassment shall be treated as having been carried out by the employer whether or not it was done with his knowledge or approval.[15] In such circumstances the employer can only escape liability if he can show that he "took such steps as were reasonably practicable to prevent the employee from doing that act or from doing, in the course of his employment, acts of that description."[16]

(3) Duty to give an employee reasonable support in performing his or her job

This will be of particular importance when one is considering workload. In situations such as in the *Walker* case it would not be difficult to find that an employer is in breach of this fundamental term of the contract of employment such that the employee can walk out and claim constructive dismissal.

Disability Discrimination Act 1995

Section 1 of the Act[17] provides that a person is disabled for the purpose of the Act if:

> "he has a physical or mental impairment which has a substantial and long term adverse effect on his ability to carry out normal day to day activities."

In *Goodwin* v *The Patent Office*,[18] the EAT has recently confirmed that this section requires a tribunal to consider the evidence in a particular case by reference to four different conditions.

(1) Does the applicant have an impairment which is either mental or physical?

(2) Does the impairment affect the applicant's ability to carry out normal day to day activities in one of the respects set out in

---

[15] SDA, s41(1), RDA, s32(1).
[16] See further under Sex and Race Discrimination.
[17] It will be noted that the Act does not apply to employers of less than 20 employees.
[18] [1999] IRLR 4; [1999] 1 DiscLR.

Schedule 1, paragraph. 4(1) and does it have an adverse effect?

(3) Is the adverse effect substantial?

(4) Is the adverse effect long-term?

Certain of these concepts require elucidation and some assistance can be derived form the Guidance issued by the Secretary of State under section 3 of the Act on 25 July 1996.[19]

Mental impairment

The definition of mental impairment is refined in Schedule 1 to the Act to include an impairment resulting from or consisting of a mental illness, providing that it is a clinically well recognised illness. Not all mental impairments will satisfy this test and some, such as alcoholism and kleptomania are specifically excluded for obvious policy reasons.

If there is any doubt as to whether a particular condition is clinically well recognised it would be advisable to consult the World Health Organisation's International Classification of Diseases which is likely to determine the issue either way.[20]

Normal day-to-day activities

What constitutes a day-to-day activity has been left unspecified and to the extent that such activities are more easily recognised than defined this must surely be correct. An impairment will, however, be taken to affect a person's ability to carry out normal day-to-day activities if it affects one of the following:

- mobility
- manual dexterity
- physical co-ordination
- continence
- ability to lift, carry, or otherwise move everyday objects
- speech, hearing or eye sight
- memory, the ability to concentrate, learn or understand
- perception of the risk of physical danger.

---

[19] SI 1996 No 1996.
[20] See para 14 of the Guidance.

Substantial adverse effects

It should be remembered that the Act is concerned with a person's "ability" to carry out day-to-day activities. Accordingly, that a person *can* carry out such activities does not mean that his *ability* to carry them out has not been impaired. What will amount to a "substantial" adverse effect is not defined in the Act but reference to the Guide suggests that it has been used in the sense of "more than minor or trivial" as opposed to "very large".

Where an applicant has been prescribed medication for his illness a tribunal may be required to consider how the applicant's abilities had actually been effected whilst he was on medication and then consider what effects there may have been but for the medication: the "deduced" effects. The question then becomes whether or not the actual or deduced effects have a more than trivial impact upon the applicant's ability to carry out normal day-to-day activities.

In the statutory Guidance the phrase "substantial condition" has been linked to the taking of medication.[21]

Long term effects

An impairment will be found to be long term if:
- it has lasted for at least 12 months
- the period for which it lasts can reasonably be expected to be 12 months
- it can reasonably be expected to last for the rest of the life of the person affected
- where an impairment ceases to have a substantial adverse effect upon a person's ability to carry out normal day-to-day activities it will be treated as continuing to have that effect if it is likely to recur.

Having considered the above guidelines it will be immediately apparent that a person suffering from stress may well fall within the definition of someone under a disability for the purposes of the Act. It is likely that someone suffering from stress such that it becomes a recognised mental illness is unlikely to remain at work, but if he does,

---

[21] Part II, para A1.

by virtue of section 4(1), it is unlawful for an employer to discriminate against him in offering new opportunities to the workforce. More importantly, section 6 imposes an obligation upon employers to make reasonable adjustments to remove any "substantial disadvantage" which a disabled employee might suffer as compared to persons who were not disabled. Examples of reasonable adjustment are provided in section 6(3) and include making adjustments to premises, assigning him to a different place of work (both important where the stressor is part of the physical surroundings), allocating some of the disabled person's duties to another person, altering work hours, allowing the person to be absent for rehabilitation, treatment and assessment, providing adequate training and supervision. A failure to make such adjustments will be held to be an act of discrimination (for which an action in damages lies) unless the employer can establish that the failure was justified.

Sex Discrimination Act 1975 and Race Relations Act 1976

Under both Acts "less favourable treatment" is prohibited whether on grounds of race or sex.[22]

Following the decision in the recent case of *Sheriff v Klyn Tugs (Lowestoft) Ltd*[23] legislation against race and sex discrimination has gained particular importance in the context of workplace stress-related claims. Discrimination, particularly in the form of harassment, is frequently cited and widely recognised as a major cause of stress and it has always been the case that damages could be awarded for injury to feelings, the best indicator often being the stress and upset which the act of discrimination had caused.[24]

The decision in *Sheriff v Klyn Tugs (Lowestoft) Ltd*[25] however, has confirmed that both an employment tribunal (pursuant to s 56, RRA) and a county court (pursuant to s 57, SDA) has the ability to award damages not only for injury to feelings but also for physical and mental injury caused as a result of the statutory torts of discrimination based on either race or sex. Since there is no longer any upper limit on the

---

[22] RDA, s(1)(a), SDA, s1(1)(a).
[23] [1999] IRLR 481.
[24] SDA, s66(4), RDA, s57(4).
[25] *Supra*, fn 23.

level of general damages which can be ordered under these Acts, claims for stress and stress-related illnesses may become increasingly common in the field of discrimination legislation.

Indeed, notwithstanding the strict time limits involved, there may well be advantages in commencing an action in an employment tribunal as opposed to a county court. First, as indicated above, damages are recoverable for injury to feelings. Clearly, there will be a substantial overlap between injury to feelings and damages for mental disorder and double recovery will not be permitted. However, where the medical evidence of a recognised and specifically defined mental illness is weak, resort to damages for injury to feelings may be of some attraction. This is particularly so given the recent increase in the level of awards made under this head. Whilst the minimum such award is only likely to be £500[26], figures available for 1998 suggest this will very often be exceeded, sometimes dramatically so.[27]

Second, unlike in an action in negligence, under the anti-discrimination legislation damage need not be reasonably foreseeable. Third, whilst in a common law action based upon an intentional tort committed by a fellow employee there is a fairly narrow test of vicarious liability, the test of "secondary liability" in discrimination law is significantly wider.[28] Fourth, the common law concept of contributory negligence (or some analogous concept) may not apply in the field of discrimination law although this has yet to be fully tested.

To date, there has been a reluctance on the part of "common lawyers" to pursue actions for personal injuries in an employment tribunal. Concern has often been raised as to the inexperience of such tribunals in handling complicated medical issues. Whilst it is correct that employment tribunals are not as used to dealing with such matters as the county and High Court, this is to do no more than state the obvious. It does not mean that they are not capable of doing so. Indeed, any perceived failing on part of an employment tribunal is more likely to reflect a failure on the part of the lawyers and medical

---

[26] The minimum amount is likely to be £500, see *Sharifi* v *Strathclyde Regional Council* [1992] IRLR 259, EAT; *Deane* v *London Borough of Ealing* [1993] IRLR 209, EAT.

[27] In 1997 the average awards were as follows: disability discrimination £1,822, race discrimination £1,632, sex discrimination £2,441. In 1998 these figures had risen to £2,534, £3,730 and £2,907 respectively (Equal Opportunities Review No 86 July/August 1999).

[28] *S T* v *North Yorkshire County Council* [1999] IRLR 81, CA.

experts to explain the position properly (and concisely). As the potential advantages of pursuing a claim (for stress caused by discrimination) in an employment tribunal as opposed to a county court reach a wider audience so will such tribunals get up to speed and the basis of present criticism diminish.

Chapter 7

The Future

An approved code of practice

Whilst the law on this topic will continue to develop on a case-by-case basis, the pace of judicial acceptance of claims based on stress in the workplace may be forced to quicken. In July 1999, in response to concerns of the Health and Safety Commission (HSC), the Health and Safety Executive (HSE) and Ministers about the increasing growth (at least in publicity terms) of stress at work, the HSE and the Occupational Health Advisory Committee (OHAC) of the HSC were asked to consider whether or not an approved Code of Practice about stress under the Health and Safety at Work 1974, and in particular the nature of an employer's duties under that Act as far as stress is concerned, should be produced.

What is an Approved Code of Practice

An Approved Code of Practice has a somewhat peculiar status in law. It seeks to give special guidance as to how the law can be complied with. Whilst it is not an offence to fail to comply with its provisions, if an employer is prosecuted for a breach of health and safety law and it is established that it has not complied with an Approved Code of Practice then, unless it is able to show that it complied with the legal requirements placed upon it in some other way, it is almost bound to be found to be at fault. The reverse position also holds, namely that compliance with an Approved Code of Practice will absolve an employer from liability.

In February 1996 the HSC published criteria which it said would need to fulfilled before an future Approved Codes of Practice would be issued. These are that:

(a) there is clear evidence of a widespread or significant problem;
(b) the overall approach being taken to an area of risk is by amplifying the general duties in the Health and Safety at Work Act or preparing goal-setting regulations;
(c) there is a strong presumption in favour of a particular method

or methods that can be amplified in an Approved Code of Practice in support of the general duties or goal-setting regulations to give authoritative practical guidance; and

(d) the alternative (if the persuasive force of an Approved Code of Practice proved to be insufficient to guide people towards the recommended methods) is likely to be more prescriptive regulation.

The publication of an Approved Code of Practice would not be the first step which either the HSE or the HSC has taken in an attempt to assist employers in dealing with stress at work. In the early 1990's the HSE commissioned an independent review of the scientific literature on stress[1] which led to the publication in 1995 of guidance on work-related stress – *Stress at Work: A Guide for Employers.*[2] This publication was supplemented in 1998 with the distribution of a free leaflet intended for small and medium-sized businesses entitled "Help on work-related stress: a short guide."[3]

Whilst no doubt a valid attempt to raise the profile of stress in the workplace, these publications have had little impact. Indeed, the HSC would perhaps be the first to admit that whilst they may have been a worthy contribution to the debate, they have done little to change employers' perceptions or current working practices. A public campaign (no doubt similar to the recent *Good Health is Good Business* campaign) is planned to help employers become more aware of the role of stress at work and what can be done to cope with and reduce it but it would seem from the discussion document which it has issued that the HSC regards this as only supplementary. The question is, supplementary to what?

The HSC considered the advice which it received from the HSE and the OHAC of the HSC and decided that the issue generated such divergence of opinion between, at one end of the debate, those who think that stress in the workplace needs to be tackled at a societal level and, at the other, those who regard stress as an individual matter depending upon how each person copes with the strains which life

---

[1] *Stress Research and Stress Management: Putting Theory to Work,* Tom Cox, CRR 61/1993, ISBN 0 7176 0648 8, HSE Books, 1993.
[2] HS(G) 116, ISBN 0 7176 0733 X HSE Books, 1995.
[3] INDG 281, HSE Books, 1998.

and, in particular life at work, place on them that it would be prudent to issue a discussion document in the hope of receiving the views from as wide an audience as possible before deciding whether or not to publish an Approved Code of Practice.

In fact, the tone of that discussion document would suggest that an Approved Code of Practice may well be some way off. The final conclusion of the HSE and the OHAC of the HSC (if they can be said to have reached a final conclusion) was that whilst some elements of guidance on stress would be amenable to an Approved Code of Practice, others would not.

A half-way house appears to have been favoured, namely a largely ordinary guidance-based document which would nevertheless contain certain segments of Approved Code of Practice status. A suggested model for such a document was included in the discussion document. The HSC has expressed concerns, however, as to whether even such a limited Approved Code of Practice would be feasible. In particular, it was felt that proving beyond reasonable doubt (we are dealing here with criminal sanctions) that:

(a) the stress was work-related,
(b) it was foreseeable and that
(c) there were clear courses of action which could have been taken to prevent it

would only be possible in the most extreme cases.

Such is the dilemma which the HSC sees itself as facing that it has even suggested limiting its action to some of the specific causes of stress, as opposed to dealing with stress as a whole. This may be easier to police effectively but is it providing the sort of protection which employees are perceived to need? Indeed, it could be argued that the HSC and HSE are not the bodies most likely to bring about a sea change in the attitude and approach of employers. Far more often than not it is the threat of litigation rather than an ad hoc visit by the HSE which concentrates employers' minds.

Accordingly, if the goal of the HSE is to regulate the workplace and to seek to reduce the impact which stress is having both upon individuals and businesses, might it not be better focusing less on the question of enforcement in the criminal courts (the success of which is not one of the criteria arrived at for the issue of an Approved Code of Practice) and more on the fact that an Approved Code of Practice would set a benchmark against which employers can be judged in the civil courts? Whilst an employer may be immune to the seemingly ever increasing focus of the national print and broadcast media on the question of stress and escape sanction as a result, ignorance of an Approved Code of Practice would not be so permitted. Might this not be a case of the HSC being unable to see the wood for the trees? The results of the discussion document are yet to be fully collated. If an Approved Code of Practice is to be issued a Consultative Document containing such a Code in draft form will precede it. Readers may be well advised not to hold their breath for either.

Index